# of a

Shepherd

Darla Noble

Through the Eyes of a Shepherd

Copyright, © 2017 Darla Noble

Printed in the United States of America. All rights reserved under International Copyright Law.
ISBN: 978-1979664790

Contents

Introduction

Spiritual insight often comes in the most unexpected way. For me, one of those ways has been the years I spent as a shepherd. Yes, the kind of shepherd that actually takes care of the sheep.

Our barns and pastures have served as my "spiritual classrooms" as I watched and cared for our sheep. I understand this might seem strange to most people—given the fact that sheep are usually thought of as mindless and dumb. After all, what could a sheep possibly teach anyone, right? Wrong!

The words on the pages of this book are the result of many of the "Oh...*now* I see what you mean" moments—moments when God used these unpretentious animals to teach me the truth of his Word and its relevance in my life...and yours.

This book is also my thank-you note to God for his willingness to get down on my level to speak to me. It is my way of fulfilling Jesus' command:

Therefore go and make disciples of all nations, baptizing them in the name of the Father and of the Son and of the Holy Spirit, and teaching them to obey everything I have commanded you. And surely I am with you always, to the very end of the age.

~Matthew 28:19–20 NIV

To my Lord and Savior, Jesus Christ: Thank you for believing I am worth talking to…worth teaching…worth saving.

To my husband, John: Thanks for all the years we spent making Generation 5 Farm the place we raised our children and working together to provide for our family.

Misconceptions

Know that the Lord is God. It is he who made us, and we are his; we are his people, the sheep of his pasture.

~Psalm 100:3 NIV

Most people are under the impression that the words "sheep" and "stupid" are synonymous. If you're one of those people, then ask yourself this question: if sheep really *are* stupid, what does that say about us — considering the many comparisons between sheep and men in the Bible? And even more importantly, what does that say about God?

Genesis 1:27 says, *"So God created man in his own image, in the image of God he created him; male and female he created them."*

Therefore, since we are created in the image of God (as the Bible says we are), *and* are called the "sheep of his pasture" (Psalm 100:3), I think I can say with a fair amount of certainty that God takes offense when sheep are viewed so unflatteringly — and falsely.

More accurately, the appropriate words to describe sheep are *trusting* and *dependent*. They recognize their shepherd and trust that he/she has their best interest at heart. Unlike many animals that are continually on the move in order to find food, sheep are content to wait on the shepherd to supply their needs.

Another characteristic of sheep, which proves their trusting nature, is the fact that sheep are born followers. Where one goes, they all go. This attribute of their character comes in handy when moving and working the flock. But it is also my job as their shepherd to be ready to step in and change their course if who or what they are following is headed for danger.

Are you beginning to see the connection between man and sheep? Can you think of a word that comes to mind to describe this connection? Let me help you out: character. That's the word we need. Or at least it should be. The sheep's instinctive character to be dependent, trusting, and to follow without hesitation are exactly the character traits God desires us to have in our relationship with him.

It is God's desire that we know he has our best interest at heart, for us to be content to depend on him to supply our needs instead of depending on worldly pleasures to provide a false sense of security and satisfaction, and for our faith in him to be strong enough to keep us focused on *his* design for our life.

So, you see, sheep aren't so baaad (sorry, I couldn't resist). As a matter of fact, they're just what the Good Shepherd is looking for.

Additional Scriptures of Encouragement

Trust in the Lord and do good; dwell in the land and enjoy safe pasture. ~Psalm 37:3 NIV

Trust in the Lord with all your heart and lean not on your own understanding; in all your ways acknowledge him, and he will make your paths straight. ~Proverbs 3:5–6 NIV

Humble yourselves, therefore, under God's mighty hand, that he may lift you up in due time. Cast all your anxiety on him because he cares for you. ~1 Peter 5:6–7 NIV

A Gift from the Heart

For God so loved the world that he gave his one and only Son, that whoever believes in him shall not perish but have eternal life. ~John 3:16 NIV

Take a moment to recall a few of the gifts you've received in your lifetime. Chances are, those that come to mind as being the most special are the ones that came from the heart of the giver.

For me, one gift that comes to mind is the homemade paper angel my thirty-one-year-old son made when he was two. He made it in Sunday school to grace the top of our Christmas tree. Zach put everything he had into coloring that paper angel. When he proudly presented it to his dad and me, I told him his angel would always be placed on the top of my tree. And it is.

That paper angel covered in yellow and blue crayon may not look like much and it may have undergone "surgery" to tape a craft stick to its back so it can remain upright, but it is more precious to me than the most costly tree-topper ever made.

Gift-giving is a ritual almost as old as time itself and one our Father, God, teaches us should come from the heart. Yes, God teaches us early on that gift-giving is something he takes seriously.

Case in point: Cain and Abel's gifts to God, which happens to be the first ever recorded gift-giving event.

Genesis chapter four gives us the account of Cain and Abel bringing gifts or offerings to God. (It is also the first time sheep are mentioned, in case you are interested.) Verse two tells us that God "found favor" with Abel's gift (offering).

Would you like to guess what that gift was? That's right. It was a lamb—one of Abel's finest lambs. But God did more than simply "find favor" with his "lamb gift." God was so impressed with Abel's choice of gift that he (God) decided to give a few "lamb gifts" of his own once in a while.

In case you aren't sure what I mean by that, let me refresh your memory…

Genesis chapter twenty-two tells us that Abraham's faith was put to the test in a BIG way. God tested Abraham to see where or if there were any perimeters to Abraham's willingness to obey. But when God saw that Abraham was willing to sacrifice his precious son, Isaac, if necessary, God sent a lamb in Isaac's place.

I don't know about you, but from a parent's point of view, there's no doubt in my mind that Abraham had never gotten *anything* he wanted more in his life than that lamb.

A lamb was also the required offering (gift) in order to keep the death angel away from the firstborn of the Israelites just prior to their exodus from Egypt.

A lamb was the preferred sacrifice or gift for numerous transgressions of the law God gave the Israelites through Moses.

When Jesus came onto the scene as an adult to begin his ministry, John the Baptist says, "Look, the Lamb or God who takes away the sins of the world!" (John 1:29 *NIV*)

Jesus was a master storyteller; he used his stories or parables to help the people understand the purpose of his ministry. Not surprisingly, several of those parables involve sheep and a shepherd. It's also no surprise that each time Jesus uses sheep in one of his parables; the sheep are cherished and valued by the shepherd. They are never seen in a negative light (Matthew 25:31–33; Matthew 18:12–14; Luke 15:3–7).

Finally, and most importantly, God gave his son to be the sacrificial lamb for our sins— yours and mine. Has there ever been a truer gift given from the heart? (1 Peter 1:18–21).

Sheep were pretty handy to have around back in the day, wouldn't you agree?

Don't worry, I'm not recommending a one-stop shopping experience at the farm nearest you. Talk about hard to wrap! But when it comes to giving gifts to our Savior, we need to remember that God isn't all that different than we are. The gifts that mean the most to him are the ones we give that come from our hearts; gifts that "cost" us ourselves. In other words, trusting God to do what is best for you instead of always taking matters into your own hands, acknowledging his blessings instead of having an attitude of self-sufficiency, and giving your heart and soul to him for all time in all things.

Additional Scriptures of Encouragement

Which of you, if his son asks for bread, will give him a stone? Or if he asks for a fish, will give him a snake? If you, then, though you are evil, know how to give good gifts to your children, how much more will your Father in heaven give good gifts to those who ask him!
~Matthew 7:9–11 NIV

But the king replied to Araunah, "No I insist on paying you for it. I will not sacrifice to the Lord my God burnt offerings that cost me nothing. ~2 Samuel 24:24 NIV

Every good and perfect gift is from above, coming down from the Father of the heavenly lights, who does not change like shifting shadows. ~James 1:17 NIV

Just Like Tillie

Be imitators of God, therefore, as dearly loved
children… ~Ephesians 5:1 NIV

Tillie. What can I say about Tillie? She's
old, content, and well-fed (it shows); trusting,
gentle, and willing to go wherever I lead her.
What a sheep! I want to be just like Tillie. Well,
maybe I'm not so anxious about the *old* part, but
the rest…well; we could all learn a thing or two
from Tillie.

Content: *Be content with what you have,*
because God has said, "Never will I leave you, never
will I forsake you." ~Hebrews 13:5 NIV

Tillie never goes beyond her boundaries
in search of "greener pastures." She doesn't need
to. As a shepherd, it's *my* responsibility to make
sure she and the other sheep have what they
need.

Making sure they are properly cared for isn't just for their sake, though, but for mine as well. If Tillie and the others are healthy and content, then they are also more productive. And if they are productive, so is the farm. You might say it's a win-win situation.

Tillie is content because her shepherd is always there to make sure she (and the rest of the flock) is satisfied with what she has.

What about you and me? How do we stack up in the contentment department?

Do we ever go searching for "greener pastures" instead of enjoying what God places before us? Or are we content to know that God, our Father and Maker, will always be there to supply our needs and more?

Well fed: *But solid food is for the mature, who by constant use have trained themselves to distinguish good from evil. ~Hebrews 5:14* NIV

You can tell by looking at her that Tillie gets her share of "solid food." But that's okay, because, in return she's doing what she's meant to do to the very best of her ability — produce strong, healthy lambs.

One of the most frequent questions we're asked in regards to raising sheep is do they need anything to eat besides grass? My husband John always answers by saying, "You can't starve a profit out of them."

What he means is that while they can *survive* on grass and hay, they won't reach their full potential without a more nutrient-filled diet. And if their performance is less than what it could be, so is our earning potential.

The same can be said about our spiritual diet. We need to make sure we are gilling up on the solid food that God's Word provides in order to live up to our potential as disciples of Jesus Christ?

So ask yourself: are you feasting at God's banquet table in order to be energized as the hands and feet of Jesus? Or are you merely surviving on what you hear on Sunday, on television, online, or by merely being "a good person"?

Trust: *When Jesus spoke again to the people, he said, "I am the light of the world. Whoever follows me will never walk in darkness, but will have the light of life." ~John 8:12* NIV

Tillie follows me wherever I go. She is also the one who leads the other sheep to where they need to be. Tillie follows because she has no reason to worry. She *trusts* that whatever I do will be for her benefit. She never balks or hesitates. She simply follows.

Why can't we be more like Tillie when it comes to obeying God? Why do we have such a hard time trusting the one who made us to make the most of our lives?

There is an old chorus we used to sing called *"Let Go and Let God Have His Wonderful Way."* I think that just about says it all.

Gentle: *Be completely humble and gentle; be patient, bearing with one another in love. ~Ephesians 4:2 NIV*

Tillie endures more than a fair amount of poking, patting, and pulling from the anxious, uncoordinated hands of children who come for farm tours throughout the year. Their squeals of excitement don't upset her. She *bears with* those who are different. She would never *not* let the children pet her. Tillie's gentle nature is proven by the fact that she doesn't have it in her to hurt anyone.

Oh, to be like Tillie — to be wise and gentle enough not to expect non-Christians to have Christ-like behavior, but being compassionate and a living example of Christ's love.

How much difference do you think it would make in your life and in the church to lovingly embrace the opportunity to teach and mentor new Christians and to love those different from us just because God does? And how glorious it would feel to never hurt or offend anyone!

Tillie may just be a sheep, but without saying a word, she speaks volumes. I want to be just like Tillie. Don't you?

Additional Scriptures of Encouragement

In the morning I lay my request before you and wait in expectation. ~Psalm 5:3 NIV

But let all who take refuge in you be glad; let them ever sing for joy. Spread your protection over them, that those who love your name may rejoice in you.
~Psalm 5:11 NIV

I am not saying this because I am in need, for I have learned to be content whatever the circumstances. I know what it is to be in need, and I know what it is to have plenty. I have learned the secret of being content in any and every situation, whether well fed or hungry, whether living in plenty or in want. I can do all everything through him who gives me strength.
~Philippians 4:11–13 NIV

Rocky Ground

*…because you know that the testing of your faith
develops perseverance. ~James 1:3* NIV

Lush green pastures complete with a
stream gently rippling over stones made smooth
by time and water…sheep scattered about
grazing contentedly without a care in the
world….an occasional 'baaaah', a little lamb
nestled against its momma…ahhhh, what peace
and tranquility.

Generally speaking that is how an artist
portrays the life of a shepherd and his (or her, in
my case) sheep. But something is missing from
this peaceful little scene. Would you like to
know what it is? A few rocks, that's what!

In order to explain my point, you'll have
to permit me to give you a brief (I promise)
lesson in "sheep podiatry."

These four-legged friends of ours have hooves that need trimming if they grow too long. It is a tedious job that can wear you out in a hurry. But it is also a job that can be avoided if you make sure the sheep spend a bit of time walking on rocks.

Rocks act as emery boards to file or wear down their hooves in order to sustain sure-footing and to guard against foot rot. (Sounds lovely, doesn't it?)

Second Corinthians 1:3–4 says: *Praise be to the God and father of our Lord Jesus Christ, the Father of compassion and the God of all comfort, who comforts us in all our troubles, so that we can comfort those in any trouble with the comfort we ourselves have received from God.*

Rocky ground (or in Paul's words, "trouble") has the same effect on us. Our rocky ground (difficulties) allows us to effectively reach out to those who are suffering and show them the truth and tangibility of God's love.

We are best able to relate to someone in life's difficult situations when we've been there ourselves. It only makes sense that we would need to personally experience these trials in order to be able to assure people of God's ability and willingness to comfort and sustain us through these times.

Think about it...if we never experienced feelings of helplessness and fear, or our heart never ached, our words of comfort to someone feeling helpless or brokenhearted would seem (and be) empty.

When we are able to relate to the pain and needs of others because of our own similar struggles, we can be a living testimony of God's mercy and strength in times of adversity. A job loss, the death of a loved one, financial setbacks, illness, divorce, rebellious children, or whatever else we've been through allows us to be the eyes, ears, feet, and hands of Jesus to those in need.

Our Christian character is built by holding tight to God's hand while we stumble across these rocky paths we travel in our lives. Who of us has learned compassion without ever reaching out to anyone? Who has learned appreciation for material blessings by being given everything they want? Who has learned self-discipline without having been disciplined?

Making our way over rocky ground may give us sore feet or even a sprained ankle, but remember — it also gives us the *privilege* of experiencing firsthand the awesomeness and reality of God's power.

Paul's understanding of this is evident when he says: *Three times I pleaded with the Lord to take it away from me. But he said to me, "My grace is sufficient for you, for my power is made perfect in weakness."* ~2 Corinthians 12:9 NIV

Allow yourself to be perfected.

Additional Scriptures of Encouragement

Remember how the Lord your God led you all the way in the desert these forty years to humble you and to test you in order to know what was in your heart, whether or not you would keep his commands.
~Deuteronomy 8:2 NIV

No discipline seems pleasant at the time, but painful. Later on, however, it produces a harvest of righteousness and peace for those who have been trained by it.
~Hebrews 12:11 NIV

Listen carefully to my words; let this be the consolation you give me. ~Job 21:2 NIV

Little Missy

No, the word is very near you; it is in your mouth and in your heart so you may obey it. ~Deuteronomy 30:14 NIV

Triplet births are a fairly normal occurrence in our flock. Yes, I know—I know what you are thinking. You are thinking, *Oh, how sweet.* Most of the time you would be right, but in this instance, think again!

During the first few days in the lives of these little threesomes, it is essential to make sure everyone gets their fair share of from mom. This means we have to pay extra-special attention to them; making sure we see them eat and whatnot. After all, there are three of them and momma can only feed two at a time, so there is always that chance that one of them won't get their fair share.

Because I'm both a shepherd *and* a mom, I leave little to chance. So at the first sign of malnutrition I take the necessary route of intervention by supplementing the smallest lamb's intake with a bottle.

It didn't take long for me to figure out that this was going to be the case with Little Missy. She was the "runt" of a set of triplets and just didn't have the strength to keep up.

A few short hours after her birth I could already see her energy level dropping; meaning bottle-feeding her would be necessary if she was going to survive. When I offered her the bottle, though, she refused. I wasn't too concerned — thinking that if I waited an hour or two she'd be hungry enough to eat just about anything.

But two hours later, Little Missy still refused the bottle. Then two *more* hours passed and she still wouldn't eat. This was NOT a good sign. Not good at all.

If she did not eat soon, she would become hypothermic and require even more care. I wasn't ready to give up, though, because (a) it was the right thing to do and (b) I had a bit of a pride thing going on—no lamb was going to refuse *my* treatment.

It went a little like this...

"Now you listen here, Little Missy, you need to take this bottle if you have any intentions of sticking around here for a very long."

No response but milk dripping out of her mouth and down her chin because she refused to swallow.

"If you know what's good for you, you're going to take this, but since you don't know and *I* do, just trust me and eat."

She didn't listen, and by the middle of the afternoon Little Missy was so weak she couldn't hold her head up.

Her stubborn determination had exceeded her physical strength. But I still wasn't ready to throw in the towel. In spite of her deteriorating health and the fact that most of the milk was now all over me, I was still confident that I would prove to be the winner in this battle of wills by inserting a feeding tube attached to a large syringe filled with milk down her throat and into her stomach. But even then Little Missy continued to fight me; biting holes in the tube and rendering it useless!

There was nothing left for me to do. A few hours later Little Missy died.

As I went about the rest of my day, I thought of how foolish Little Missy had been for refusing my help…for refusing life. And in the midst of my thoughts, God repeatedly brought to my mind Matthew 13:22: *The one who received the seed that fell among the thorns is the man who hears the word, but the worries of this life and the deceitfulness of wealth choke it, making it unfruitful.*

How many people do we know are like Little Missy — those who know Jesus but refuse to take what he has to offer; refusing to allow him to work in their lives and adamantly fight against him when he puts his loving arms around them?

How often are *we* guilty of being like Little Missy? We want to do things *our* way! *We* know what is best for us (or at least we think we do)! How often do we fight against the will of God for our lives and wind up at a dead end?

Don't let pride and selfishness entangle your heart; robbing you of being nourished by the Good Shepherd.

Jesus tells us that he is the way, the truth, and the life. So take every opportunity given you to feed on the Word, go to him in prayer, worship him, and enjoy the fellowship of your brothers and sisters in Christ. In other words, don't end up like Little Missy by refusing to be fed by the Good Shepherd

Additional Scriptures of Encouragement

Pride goes before destruction, a haughty spirit before a fall. ~Proverbs 16:18 NIV

He has taken me to the banquet hall, and his banner over me is love.
~Song of Songs 2:4 NIV

When Moses finished reciting all these words to all Israel, he said to them, "Take to heart all the words I have solemnly declared to you this day, so that you may command your children to obey carefully all the words of this law. They are not just idle words for you – they are your life. By them you will live long in the land you are crossing the Jordan to possess."
~Deuteronomy 32:45–47 NIV

Our Intended Purpose

*Just as each of us has one body with many members,
and these members do not all have the same function,
so in Christ we who are many form one body, and
each member belongs to all the others. We have
different gifts, according to the grace given us.*
~Romans 12:4–6a NIV

Over the last few years, I have had several experiences with the sheep that would do justice to this topic, but none is quite like the story of my daughter Olivia's experience with a bottle calf named Albert.

Albert was a calf born to one of my milk cows. He was a summer calf, so he was still being bottle-fed when the county fair rolled around. So my four-year-old daughter Olivia, who had given Albert his name, decided she was going to take him to the fair

We had no objections to her plan because we were going to be there anyway because our two older children would be showing livestock. What was one more animal in the trailer? Besides, because Albert would need his bottles, having him with us instead of having to go home to feed him would actually make it easier on us. We also figured it would be a good experience for her.

Since Albert was a "bottle baby," we knew he would pose no problems in the show ring. Olivia would have to do nothing more than pick up the rope attached to his halter to make him go wherever she went. She and Albert were quite a hit in the show ring, and he "did her proud."

The fair came and went, and before we knew it, almost a year had passed. The time had come for Albert to fulfill his *intended purpose* and become food for our family.

Our two older children, aged six and nine at the time, fully understood the purpose of the livestock on the farm and weren't bothered by the fact that something they had helped care for often ended up on the table. But Olivia, well, Olivia was a bit more sensitive. We just weren't sure if she would be as understanding.

She did pretty well when we left Albert at the processing plant. We told her he was staying there to be made into meat for our family. She understood the concept of what we were saying but remained quiet during the ride home.

Over the next few days, she talked about missing him, but he had gotten large enough and aggressive enough that she had not been tending to him for quite a while, so it wasn't as if she had lost a buddy that followed her around the barnyard. By the time we picked up the packaged meat, we felt fairly certain she had come to terms with what had taken place. Or had she?

The evening after we picked up the meat from the processor, I fixed hamburgers for supper—courtesy of Albert. After taking a couple of bites of her hamburger, little Olivia looked up and asked, "Is this Albert?"

John and I exchanged quick glances. We were both unsure of how Olivia would "take the news." But John, not wavering from the truth, gently but firmly replied, "Yes, Olivia, it is."

Without missing a beat, and wearing a big grin, Olivia swallowed and said with unabashed enthusiasm, "He tastes pretty good, don't he!"

Wouldn't life be great if it was that easy for us to appreciate and understand what *our* intended purpose is! But unlike Albert, we have too many options…or so we think.

The frustration we often feel in regards to knowing what career to pursue, where to live, or what we're supposed to be doing for God, isn't from God's lack of ability to lead us, but in our lack of ability to follow God's leading.

We make something difficult out of something that is really relatively simple.

Jeremiah 29:11 says: *"For I know the plans I have for you," declares the Lord, "plans to prosper you and not harm you, plans to give you hope and a future."*

Do you understand what God is saying? He has a plan—an intended purpose for YOU.

Yes, God has an "intended purpose" for each of us. We are all created to fulfill a specific purpose in his plan for the world. It is a purpose he is willing to reveal to you. All you have to do is ask. Ask in prayer, listen in prayer and Bible study, and be open to the people and circumstances around you. If you do, he promises to show you just what it is he has in mind for you. And you can be sure it will be everything you could possibly ask for…and more!

Additional Scriptures of Encouragement

In his heart a man plans his course, but the Lord

determines his steps.

~ Proverbs 16:9 NIV

Now all has been heard; here is the conclusion of the

matter: Fear God and keep his commandments, for

this is the whole duty of man. ~Ecclesiastes 12:13

NIV

I will instruct you and teach you in the way you

should go; I will counsel you and watch over you.

~Psalm 32:8 NIV

Personally Interested

To the man belong the plans of the heart, but from the Lord comes the reply of the tongue. ~*Proverbs 16:1*
NIV

Q. What's the difference between a noise and a sound?

A. It depends on who you are.

To some, the cries of an infant are an annoyance—aka noise. To others, these same cries are the song of life. The same can be said about the bawling and baahing that takes place around our farm just after feeding time.

To an outsider (i.e., anyone besides our family), the sound of a few hundred ewes calling their lambs back to them, combined with the sound of almost twice as many lambs calling for "mom"—all at the same time is, well, annoying and loud.

Our household would readily agree with the loud part, but we'd replace the "annoying" with "amazing." I know — sounds a bit strange, but bear with me a minute and I'll tell you why.

What makes it so amazing is the fact that just like a mother can distinguish the cries of her child from the other babies in the church nursery or in a park full of other children, ewes can distinguish the cries of their lambs from among the masses.

Equally amazing is the fact that just as a child knows its mother's voice from the very beginning, the lambs can distinguish their mother's voice equally well.

So…after the ewes have eaten, it takes very little time with virtually no confusion, before everyone is reunited and all is well. Day after day it's the same. But in spite of the predictability of their actions, I never grow tired of these daily "family reunions."

Watching the lambs take refuge close to their mothers' side; being welcomed by gentle motherly nudges and listening as stillness settles over the flock is reassuring and gives me a sense of peace.

This reassurance is the voice of God speaking to my heart, reminding me that no matter where I am, or how many of his children are crying out to him at any given time, he hears *me*. And not only does he *hear* me, but he is personally interested in who I am, how I feel, and what I have to say.

Each time I call out to him I am welcomed into his presence with the knowledge that my voice is a sound he longs to hear. It is never an annoying noise. I also know without a doubt that he will never *not* recognize my voice.

The same is true for you, too. You can rest assured that no matter where you are, or how many of his children are crying out to him at any given time, he hears *you*. And just like with me, God is personally interested in who you are, how you feel, and what you have to say. Your voice is always a welcome sound to his ears and not an annoying noise.

Q. How much "music" are you making?

Additional Scriptures of Encouragement

The Lord is gracious and compassionate, slow to anger and rich in love.
~ Psalm 145:18 NIV

Ask and it will be given to you; seek and you will find; knock and the door will be opened to you.
~Matthew 7:7 NIV

And will not God bring about justice for his chosen ones, who cry out to him day and night? Will he keep putting them off? ~Luke 18:7 NIV

Never Alone

*I call on you, O God, for you will answer me; give ear
to me and hear my prayer.*
~Psalm 17:6 NIV

The calendar said it was February, but it
felt more like mid-spring, so John and I decided
to take advantage of the day and fix some fence.
We were working in a field adjacent to where
some ewes and their lambs were laying in the
sun—also enjoying the respite from winter.

But if the day wasn't already perfect
enough, God decided to use it to remind me that
when we feel separated from him, or start to feel
like our prayers are falling on deaf ears, it's not
because God doesn't hear us—and even
answering. It is because either *we're* not
listening, or seeing the answers he has given.

Here is what happened…

From where we were working I could see the water tank the sheep used for drinking, so I couldn't help but notice when one of the ewes came to get a drink with her lambs trailing beside her.

As she drank, her lambs started playing and were soon so engrossed in what they were doing they didn't notice when mom turned and walked away.

As she was walking back to rejoin the flock, she called her lambs to her. They didn't hear her, though, because they weren't paying any attention. She called again. No answer. The third time, she called as if to say, "This is the last time I'm going to tell you…" but the lambs were still too engrossed in what they were doing to pay any attention to her.

True to "her word" of having given a final warning, the momma rejoined the rest of the ewes and calmly lay back down to enjoy the sunshine.

She did so, however, without ever taking her eye off her lambs. She watched them as they continued to explore their surroundings and she watched as they almost simultaneously looked up and realized momma was no longer there and they didn't know where she was.

If I failed to see the uncertainty in the eyes of those two lambs, I certainly couldn't have missed the fear in their voices when they began to "baah" for all they were worth. They just stood there calling for mom at the top of their lungs.

But mom didn't answer. Nope, not one sound did she make. She just sat there silently and without moving a muscle, yet never taking her eye off them. Was she being negligent? No. Was she uncaring? No. Like any good mother, she was safely and reasonably allowing her children to face the consequences of their actions. This was her way of disciplining them.

But even mothers in the animal kingdom have their limits, so the moment the lambs' cries of uncertainty and fear turned to sheer panic, she stood up and simply but loudly called her lambs to her. Just one short, loud "baaaah."

That was all it took. The lambs' reaction was swift and immediate and in no time at all the little family was happily reunited.

Needless to say, the fence building had been put on hold because John and I had both given our full attention to the scene unfolding in front of us.

The lesson God placed before us in those few brief moments, though, is as real and applicable now as it was that day. The lesson: God never leaves us alone.

During this particular time in our lives, John and I were struggling with the fact that our oldest child was discovering the world as an adult for the first time.

This was unchartered territory for us, and, quite truthfully, in some ways, it wasn't going all that well— meaning, we weren't happy with some of the choices being made.

Most parents encounter this particular struggle when it comes to raising their children and sending them off into the world. We knew that. But knowing didn't make it hurt any less. And I have to confess that at the time, I was struggling with the question of why God wasn't making things turn out the way I hoped and prayed they would. Why was God ignoring me? But in those few brief moments, God explained it all…loud and clear.

Walking with God is a choice he gives us. So is the choice of *not* walking with him. When we cease to listen and be attentive, like the lambs did, God hasn't deserted us. He is simply waiting and watching for us to come to our senses.

Just like that old ewe, he never takes his eye off us, and when we're ready, he will welcome us back with open and loving arms without any hesitation.

"Okay, God, I get it," I said. In that moment, I was reminded that God loves my children even more than I do and that he is watching over them even when I can't.

How many times do we find ourselves in similar situations—accusing God of not hearing or caring about us? When we don't get the instant gratification society has led us to believe we deserve, we accuse God of not caring. We take matters into our own hands and go looking for satisfaction and gratification in other places—only to be deeply disappointed. And then when things get rough, we panic and frantically call on God to get us out of the mess we made.

We cannot justifiably put the blame on God. We have to be held responsible and accountable for the consequences of withdrawing from God's protection. But God is always faithful—always. And he is always ready to call us back into his presence. All we have to do is listen.

Additional Scriptures of Encouragement

I call on you, O God, for you will answer me; give ear to me and hear my prayer.

~Psalm 17:6 NIV

But seek first his kingdom and his righteousness, and all these things will be given to you as well.

~Matthew 6:33 NIV

Have I not commanded you? Be strong and courageous. Do not be terrified; do not be discouraged, for the Lord your God will be with you wherever you go. ~Joshua 1:9 NIV

Carried in the Shepherd's Arms

He tends his flock like a shepherd: He gathers the lambs in his arms and carries them close to his heart; he gently leads those that have young. ~ Isaiah 40:11

NIV

During winter lambing, if it is very cold outside (the temperatures are much below freezing) and/or there is snow on the ground, I scoop the newborn lambs up in my arms shortly aver they are born and start walking from to the "nursery" area of the barn. This is where the ewe and her lambs will be checked over, the lambs will be tagged for identification, and the ewe can dry her lambs off in a nice (fairly) warm environment, and feed them (if she hasn't already done so). In short, the new family is given the chance to get acquainted before being turned back out into the flock.

Now I know you're probably thinking it's not very wise on my part to interfere with an animal and her newborn young. And, in the case of most animals, you would be right. But sheep are different. While they *do* possess motherly instincts, they are not, by nature, an aggressive animal—especially around someone they trust. So, thankfully the ewe's maternal instinct, combined with her trust in me, motivates her to follow close behind; allowing the transfer to take place in a matter of mere minutes and without any problems.

Well, *usually* that's the way it happens…but not always.

Sometimes patience and coaxing (on my part) are involved. Sometimes I have to hold the lambs just out of reach, wait for the ewe to come forward and realize the lamb is hers, take a few more steps (walking backwards), wait some more, take a few more steps, wait…well, you get the picture.

This reluctance generally stems from a first-time mom's nervousness. Once in a while, that reluctance even turns into refusal. When that happens — which thankfully isn't often — I've been known to put on quite a rodeo. But eventually I always get everyone where they need to be, and once in the barn, things quickly settle down. Only then can I be satisfied with the knowledge that I have done my job in making sure that both the lambs and ewes receive the care and attention they need.

One morning, as I was carrying lambs to the barn, as God has so often done, he allowed the Scriptures to speak directly to me. This time, it was the words of Isaiah 40:11 that came to mind: *He tends his flock like a shepherd: He gathers the lambs in his arms and carries them close to his heart; he gently leads those that have young.*

I love it when God does that. It is such a comfort to experience firsthand the truth of God's Word.

To appreciate on a deeper level, the depth of his desire to parent us by holding us close to his heart and cover us with his abundant wisdom and mercy as he leads us through life — well, it's nothing short of incredible.

But in thinking about this, I had to ask myself what kind of leader I was as a mom. Was I doing enough to lead our four children to seek out a personal relationship with Jesus Christ? I also had to ask how good of a job I was doing at following my Savior. Did my life reflect who I said I was?

Both are questions every parent needs to ask themselves. Do we willingly follow God's Word in regards to raising our children or do we resist — even wrestle against him — by following the philosophies of whoever is most popular or makes us most comfortable?

As a mother of four and shepherd to a few hundred, I am reminded daily that there is no one more qualified to instruct us in how to care for our children than the one who made them in the first place—our Father, God. The Good Shepherd.

Additional Scriptures of Encouragement

If any of you lacks wisdom, he should ask God, who gives generously to all without finding fault, and it will be given to him. ~James 1:5 NIV

Discipline your son, and he will give you peace; he will bring delight to your soul. ~Proverbs 29:17 NIV

When I said, "My foot is slipping," your love, O Lord, supported me. ~Psalm 94:18 NIV

The Facts of Life

Do not let this Book of the Law depart from your mouth; meditate on it day and night, so that you may be careful to do everything written in it. Then you will be prosperous and successful. ~Joshua 1:8 NIV

Fact number one: There comes a time in every lamb's life that it must be weaned away from its mother.

Fact number two: There is a wrong way and a right way to accomplish this task.

The wrong way is to pick a day convenient for *us* to sort out the lambs and separate them from the ewes. The result in doing it this way is pure chaos! The noise and stress levels are over the top. Mothers bawling for babies, babies bawling for their mothers — non-stop and virtually nonstop for two or three days! Like I said…pure chaos.

Sometimes the stress level is so intense that a lamb (or lambs) quit eating and lose weight. There have even been a few cases in which the lambs have actually died for no other reason that stress.

It doesn't take a genius to understand why we don't use this method of weaning, does it? Doing so would be nearly as detrimental to us as it would be the sheep. So instead, we do it the right way.

The right way to wean is to sort out the lambs and move the ewes to a different pasture; leaving the lambs where they are — in familiar territory. Oh, and most importantly, it must be done on a day the almanac says is a good day to do it — a day on which the moon is in the proper phase to perform such a task.

Yes, that's right, the signs of the moon! Who'd a thunk, it! But as it turns out, the "old timers" knew what they were talking about after all. There really is something to this moon stuff.

I know it sounds strange—even a little crazy—but I've seen it with my own eyes and heard it with my own ears.

When we wean by the almanac, the process is one that can be described as peaceful and quiet. No noise. Nothing out of the ordinary, that is.

Weight loss and sickness? These things are not an issue. Death? Again, not an issue. Don't laugh. I have no idea how or why it works, I just know it does!

Fact number three: There is a right way and a wrong way to live life.

Fact number four: Each one of us is given the choice as to which way we chose to go.

God gives us free choice. We can live life doing things our way by working where we want to work, living where and how we want to live, going where we want to go, and doing what we want to do.

We go about our business thinking we've got this life thing all figured out until something goes wrong (and it will). That's when we fall apart.

At the first signs of stress, chaos, and upheaval, we start running. We start looking for ways to fill our hearts and lives.

We start looking for the next best thing, expecting it to magically make everything bad in our lives disappear.

But no matter how long and hard we search, we don't find what we're looking for because we aren't looking in the right place. In other words, living this way doesn't work too well.

Our other option is to put our faith in God—the one who made us and knows *the* perfect plan for our life and how to work in, and in spite of the choices we make. This is the best option to take. It's the only option if you are serious about your relationship with God.

By seeking God's guidance through prayer, Bible study and worship, we can be certain that our life will be everything we could want and more.

Allowing God to execute his plan for our life doesn't guarantee a life free from pain, worry, or heartache—just like the anxiety of separation at weaning time doesn't magically disappear because we use the almanac. That's right—the anxiety is still there, but something else is, too. I can't see it, explain it, or tell you anything else about it other than I know it is there because I've experienced it. It comforts and settles them. It eases their anxiety.

In my opinion, this is just one more piece of evidence as to why we are referred to as God's sheep. Doing things in God's way and in his time is our almanac, so to speak. Living life this way doesn't make us immune to hardships, but it *guarantee* comfort, contentment, and freedom from anxiety.

Additional Scriptures of Encouragement

I can do everything through him who gives me strength. ~Philippians 4:13 NIV

Many are the plans in a man's heart, but it is the Lord's purpose that prevails.
~Proverbs 19:21 NIV

Each one should use whatever gift he has received to serve others, faithfully administering God's grace in its various forms. ~1 Peter 4:10 NIV

Special Ethel

But God demonstrates his own love for us in this:
While we were still sinners, Christ died for us.
~Romans 5:8 NIV

Fall/winter lambing was well underway. In keeping with my morning routine on this particular day, I was walking through the field checking for lambs that had been born in the night. I hadn't gone very far when I noticed Ethel (one of the ewes we showed in fairs) with a single lamb at her side.

I was surprised to see just one, because she'd always had twins in the past. Oh, well, I thought, the lamb was stocky, alert, and had beautiful markings. From where I stood, it was the picture of health. But then the lamb turned its head to reveal the fact that the lamb was partially blind.

After examining the lamb and finding her in otherwise perfect health, I still felt inclined to get rid of her.

How would she ever survive? How would she be able to see well enough to keep up with her mother among nearly two hundred other lambs and their mothers?

It really was for the best, wasn't it? I kept asking myself this question while finishing up my chores.

Just when I had decided that getting rid of the lamb was the best thing to do, Ethel told me I was wrong.

As I stood there watching the pair, I saw Ethel give her lamb a little nudge to turn the lamb in the right direction before walking away. Without missing a beat, the lamb walked (limped) right along beside her. And when they stopped, she had no trouble figuring out how to enjoy an extended breakfast.

As I stood watching Ethel and her daughter, who quickly became known to us as Special Ethel, it became clear to me that Ethel understood her lamb would need a little extra attention, *and* that Ethel was up to the task of giving it to her.

What was even more amazing to me was the fact that Special Ethel, less than twelve hours old, already knew how to compensate for her handicap by turning, so that she could see out of her good eye.

Over the next few weeks, I couldn't look at those two (who were always side by side) without being reminded of how similar we are to Special Ethel and thanking God for putting her in my life.

In doing so, God taught me that in spite of being blessed with more than we need, and in spite of appearing to have it all together, none of us is without imperfection.

We are all spiritually handicapped; carrying around a load of imperfection. But that doesn't matter to God. Just like Special Ethel, had "Momma Ethel", we have someone who loves us in spite of our sin and imperfection and who is willing to give us the extra attention we need to make it in this life. We have a Savior who gave his life as compensation for our handicap (sin).

So who did who a favor? Initially, I thought I was doing Special Ethel a favor by 'letting' her live. But the truth of the matter is that Special Ethel was the one doing all the favors.

She opened my eyes to the extent of God's grace and mercy on each of us. She reminded me that there is nothing I can do to deserve God's love…his grace…his mercy…his gift of salvation and eternal life. Those things are mine simply because God wants to give them to me. That's all.

Additional Scriptures of Encouragement

I have been crucified with Christ and I no longer live, but Christ lives in me. The life I live in the body, I live by faith in the Son of God, who loved me and gave himself for me. ~Galatians 2:20 NIV

It does not, therefore, depend on man's desire or effort, but on God's mercy.
~Romans 9:16 NIV

Praise the Lord, O my soul, and forget not all his benefits – who forgives all your sins and heals all your diseases… ~Psalm 103:2–3 NIV

I Do It Anyway...I Have To

Keep me safe, O God, for in you I take refuge. ~Psalm 16:1 NIV

There are days when I do *not* want to go to the barn—days when the temperature is well below zero and the wind is howling.

There are days I'd rather stay inside where it is cozy and dry—days it is raining so hard it hurts when it hits my skin and soaks through every layer of clothing before I even get to the barn.

There are days I don't want to go outside because it's cold enough to have rendered the frost-proof hydrants NOT frost-proof.

There are days when I am so congested I can barely breathe—especially when I bend over to feed hay, fill water tanks, and such.

There are days when I can think of a hundred other things I would rather do than clean the lambing pens to.

But I can't let any of these things stop me from doing what I have to do. So no matter how I *feel*, I do it anyway. I have to. It's my job.

I do it because when John and I chose the field of agriculture (no pun intended), we made a commitment. We made the commitment to tend and care for the sheep — no matter what.

Being a shepherd isn't a hobby. It's not something I can do when I have a few minutes to spare or a rare leisurely afternoon. Being a shepherd is a way of life. As a shepherd, I don't have the luxury of a spontaneous weekend getaway. Much planning goes into the rare occasion that we are all gone at the same time.

I also don't have the option of hibernating inside when a snowstorm hits. If I did, my flock would soon perish and I…wouldn't be worth anything as a shepherd.

During those times when I am less than thrilled with what I'm doing, I think of how God must sometimes feel when he looks at me. I wonder...

Does he ever tire of helping me? Or would he rather be spending his time doing something besides helping me out of the mess *I* made instead of doing things his way? Are there times when he'd rather do something else besides listen to me whine and complain? Does God ever want a weekend getaway?

Thankfully, the answer to those questions is a resounding "NO!" The answer is no, because t's not in God's nature to turn his back on us.

Think about it. If God was willing to orchestrate the death of his only son for *our* benefit, which is exactly what he did, then I am confident he will never ignore us. He invested his flesh and blood into my life. Into yours. He's not about to quit on us now — or ever.

My investment (emotional and financial) in my sheep doesn't even begin to compare to his investment in his sheep (that would be us). The purpose of my flock doesn't lend itself to the need of my having an emotional attachment to them. But God's investment, well, as the Wizard of Oz would say, that's a horse of a different color.

It is impossible for God to *not* love, *not* care, and *not* listen. His love for us is too deep and too strong. It is completely unconditional. And for that I am *very* thankful.

Additional Scriptures of Encouragement

Those who know your name will trust in you, for you, Lord, have never forsaken those who seek you.
~Psalm 9:10 NIV

But because of his great love for us, God, who is rich in mercy, made us alive in Christ even when we were dead in transgressions — it is by grace you have been saved.
~Ephesians 2:4–5 NIV

This is how God showed his love among us: He sent his one and only Son into the world that we might live through him. ~1 John 4:9 NIV

Weary, Weak, and Spent

*Come to me, all you who are weary and burdened,
and I will give you rest.* ~ *Matthew 11:28* NIV

Drought is no stranger to the Midwest. It seriously affects farmers and their livestock and crops. Over the years we experienced our share of drought-related problem, but one summer several years ago, our problems were particularly severe. What little grass there had been that summer was long gone. The ground was literally burned to a crisp.

There had been no rain for several weeks, and none was expected for several more, so the chances of there being any significant changes in the condition of our pastures were slim, at best.

Not only were things dangerously dry, but the temperatures were dangerously high. It was over one-hundred degrees every day.

We were taking extra care to ration what little there was to eat in the fields by moving the sheep to "greener" pastures every day and supplementing their diet with a mix of minerals and vitamins in an effort to keep them safe and healthy. But for some, even our best efforts simply were not enough.

You see, sheep are a lot like we are when they are under a lot of stress. The combination of the intense heat and lack of proper nourishment caused the sheep to buckle under the stress. I mean literally buckle.

One day as we were leading a large group of ewes to a different field, several of them were so weak from the heat and anemia brought on by nutritional deficiencies that they collapsed. They simply could not take another step.

Sadly, some of them succumbed to their weakness and died. Others, however, lay weary and spent in need of their shepherd's tender, loving care.

At this point some of you may be asking yourself how or why we allowed things to get to that point—a reasonable question from someone not familiar with sheep. So let me take a minute to give you another quick lesson in sheep physiology.

When sheep are stressed, their digestive systems go haywire. Sound familiar? But instead of getting an ulcer, the sheep's digestive system is invaded by parasites (worms). I know…yuk!

These parasites literally begin sucking the life out of the sheep by depleting their blood supply to basically nothing. They actually rob the sheep of the *ability* to get the nutritional value out of the food they eat.

But here's the thing: this doesn't happen overnight. The symptoms don't even display themselves until considerable damage has been done—usually irreversible damage.

In other words, we weren't being neglectful shepherds. We were shepherds dealing with a crisis.

So what did we do? We gave our sheep the care they needed. My husband, my son, and I literally carried the weak and weary ewes to the shade, cooled them off, and provided them with some extra TLC in order to give them time to rest and recuperate.

Carrying these ewes was no easy task, though. Weighing in at over a hundred pounds, these girls were heavy. And we're not talking about walking a few feet. We're talking a pretty fair distance.

But as we worked to save the sheep I wasn't thinking about that. I was focusing on the task at hand and hoping the losses would be minimal. I was also praying for rain…soon.

Later that evening, as well as many times since then, I have replayed that day over in my mind. And would you like to know what I think about when I do?

I think about how weak and weary and completely spent and helpless I am at times.

I think about the times I have wanted to lie down and not get back up.

I think about how easy it can be to start feeling sorry for yourself and to try to survive on a diet of unhealthy emotions.

I think about how we sometimes try to survive in spite of the fact that the world is sucking life from us, trying to get us to buy off on false senses of happiness and fulfillment.

But they all fall short. These things are like grass burned to crisp by the sun.

These things leave us in a spiritual drought—parched and dry and starving for love, contentment, joy, and peace of mind.

I think about how we allow sin to take up residence in our hearts and minds. We allow it to silently and shrewdly suck the life out us, appearing as if we have life all figured out until it's too late (or almost too late).

I think about how thankful I am that my Savior and my Shepherd is always there to carry me to the shade and give me what I need to recuperate.

He is always there; ready to carry me when I fall. He is always there to provide for my physical needs even when I think I am on my own.

He is always there revealing the wisdom in his answers to my prayers.

He is always there to speak to me through his Word, through others, and through the promptings of the Holy Spirit. He is always there and always will be.

God is always present, always watching, always ready to pick us up, always longing for us to choose to allow him to carry us close to his heart to the life he designed us to live.

The question is: will we allow ourselves to be carried in his arms?

Additional Scriptures of Encouragement

The Lord will fight for you; you need only to be still. ~Exodus 14:14 NIV

Do not withhold your mercy from me, Lord; may your love and faithfulness always protect me. ~Psalm 40:11 NIV

For he guards the course of the just and protects the way of his faithful ones. ~Proverbs 2:8 NIV

Showing Sheep

Your beauty should not come from outward adornment, such as elaborate hairstyles and the wearing of gold jewelry or fine clothes. Rather, it should be that of your inner self, the unfading beauty of a gentle and quiet spirit, which is of great worth in God's sight. ~1 Peter 3:3–4 NIV

A few years ago, I decided it was time for our grown children to take possession of their belongings, which were still tucked away in their former bedrooms and in the attic of our house. Among those belongings were boxes of ribbons and trophies won by showing sheep and other livestock and various other 4-H projects at the county and state fairs.

As a farm family, every summer found us participating in fairs.

The work that went into getting ready for these fairs wasn't easy, but the lessons learned by our children in regards to responsibility, hard work, fairness, and gracious "sportsmanship" were worth every bit of the work and more. The most important lesson of all was the lesson of authenticity.

It was always obvious which kids were there showing livestock (sheep, cattle, etc.) that best represented the attributes of the particular animal (aka working animals) versus which kids were there showing animals they raised specifically and solely for the purpose of bringing to the fair.

We were in group number one, or as I always said, "We show sheep, but we don't have show sheep."

In other words, our sheep weren't babied, fed special feeds, painted to cover up coat "imperfections," and other such tactics.

Our sheep were fed the same thing the rest of the flock always ate, and they were washed with baby shampoo or dish soap before going on the trailer. That's all.

Did the "show sheep" look nicer? Sometimes. Did the "show sheep" act better for the judges? Not normally. You see, the way the sheep react in the ring is largely dependent on how much trust they have in the one leading them. In our case, this was almost never a problem. But for the children who didn't regularly tend to their sheep, it was a problem, because of the lack of trust the sheep had in the one leading them. Did the "show sheep" win out over the sheep we merely brought out of the flock to show? Sometimes. It depended on the judges and what they were looking for.

So...what in the world could this possibly have to do with living the life God calls us to live? So glad you asked.

In spite of the fact that we are proclaimed followers of Jesus Christ, we are often guilty of putting on a show for others. We fall prey to society's demands to look and act a certain way and to pursue a certain standard of living instead of being content to be a neat and clean representation of the "flock."

Or maybe we say all the right words, words like "holy," "righteousness," "service," "accountability group," "born again," and "fellowship," but are ignorant to what the Word of God really has to say on the subject of sin, salvation, grace, faith, and obedience.

Or maybe you make sure you go to church every Sunday (and maybe even midweek services), put a few dollars in the offering plate, donate canned goods each Christmas, and listen to Christian radio stations—you know; all the things people can see that will make them think you are a Christian.

But at home, you and your husband don't speak, your children are rebellious and disobedient, and you are successfully (for now) keeping your gambling habit a secret.

God doesn't want "show sheep." He wants sheep he can trust to present themselves as true representatives of the Church. He wants sheep who will trust the Good Shepherd to lead them through life for the purpose of being light and salt to a fallen world.

Be careful not to be a Christian in name only, because it sounds and looks good. Don't worry about covering up your flaws and imperfections. Let God show you how beautiful these things can be when he is allowed to use them for his kingdom's work. Don't try to survive on a diet of material possessions to make life shinier and more appealing. Instead, trust in the Lord to make you content in him.

Be real. Be genuine. Be authentic.

Additional Scriptures for Encouragement

For we are God's handiwork, created in Christ Jesus to do good works, which God prepared in advance for us to do. ~Ephesians 2:10 NIV

You do not delight in sacrifice, or I would bring it; you do not take pleasure in burnt offerings. My sacrifice, O God, is a broken spirit; a broken and contrite heart
you, God, will not despise. ~Psalm 51:16–17

But in your hearts revere Christ as Lord. Always be prepared to give an answer to everyone who asks you to give the reason for the hope that you have. But do this with gentleness and respect, keeping a clear conscience, so that those who speak maliciously against your good behavior in Christ may be ashamed of their slander. ~1 Peter 3:15–16

The Lord Is My Shepherd

The Lord is my shepherd; I shall not want. He maketh me to lie down in green pastures: he leadeth me beside the still waters. He restoreth my soul: he leadeth me in the paths of righteousness for his name's sake. Yea, though I walk through the valley of the shadow of death, I will fear no evil: for thou art with me; thy rod and thy staff they comfort me. Thou preparest a table before me in the presence of mine enemies: thou anointest my head with oil; my cup runneth over. Surely goodness and mercy shall follow me all the days of my life: and I will dwell in the house of the Lord forever. ~Psalm 23 KJV

One of the most quoted passages of the Scripture, the Twenty-third Psalm, records the spiritual journey of David. But it will hopefully be our spiritual journey, too.

The opening line is a confession of faith. It is the acknowledgement of who Jesus is and that life is only complete in him.

Following the confession of faith, we see that David struggled in giving everything over to God just like we do. He was *made* to lie down. He had to be *led* and *restored* to righteousness in order to remain in the presence of God. But somewhere in all that leading, David begins to grow and to change.

He realizes a life without Jesus (the Shepherd) leads to death. He understands there is evil, but that he does not need to fear its guises, because the Shepherd's rod and staff are there to comfort and save. The rod and staff of the Good Shepherd is a guide for living. It is what holds us accountable. It is what pricks our conscience and encourages us to walk the straight and narrow. It is the Word of God.

Before I go any further, I want to take a moment to explain the purpose of the shepherd's staff or rod.

The staff (that big stick with the hook on the end) is a valuable instrument to a shepherd. It is one that serves many purposes.

A shepherd's staff can be used to prod the sheep along when moving them from pasture to pasture. A shepherd might nudge a resistant animal to cross a fence or take a path unknown to them. A shepherd will often use the crooked end of their staff to retrieve sheep from danger.

It is also used to reconcile a lamb with its mother when newborn or very young lambs get "lost" in the crowd of lambs born in close proximity to one another at or about the same time.

And finally, a shepherd will use the crook of their staff to catch a sheep and lambs to examine.

While we still use staffs, a shepherd without a staff wasn't much of a shepherd back in the day. Without it, they were unable to fully protect and bring comfort to their flock.

Once David knew the value of being one with God, he was able to enjoy being in God's presence. He was able to enjoy sitting at God's table of blessings. He was willing to be anointed or recognized as one of God's sheep. He understood that the life God desires to give is overflowing with good.

Finally, David accepts the gift of salvation that comes through and by the grace and mercy of the Good Shepherd. He willingly and thankfully acknowledges that by submitting to the shepherd's leading, he will have eternal life with God.

David's spiritual journey took him to war, near-death experiences, conspiracies, adultery, tragedy, sorrow, triumph, joy, love, repentance, being a part of God's miraculous works, and most of all to the point of totally giving himself over to God.

Where is your spiritual journey taking you?

Additional Scriptures of Encouragement

The Lord is my strength and my shield; my heart trusts in him, and he helps me. My heart leaps for joy, and with my song I praise him. ~Psalm 28:7 NIV

May the God of hope fill you with all joy and peace as you trust in him, so that you may overflow with hope by the power of the Holy Spirit. ~Romans 15:13 NIV

Trust in the Lord with all your heart and lean not on your own understanding; in all your ways submit to him and he will make your paths straight. ~Proverbs 3:5–6 NIV

It's Personal

My sheep listen to my voice; I know them, and they
follow me ~John 10:27 NIV

One year, John and I decided to give each of our children a ewe (momma sheep). Our three oldest children were old enough to tell us which one they wanted.

Our youngest, Emma, was barely a year old, so her vocabulary was limited. Her ability to choose, however, was not. The one Emma chose was a small, deep red ewe that was equally drawn to her. The name my daughter chose for her was Eve.

The fact that Emma was so young and still learning to pronounce her words properly could possibly mean that the name Eve was actually her version of the word "sheep."

It doesn't matter, though, because all Eve had to do was hear Emma's voice and she came running. Emma did not even have to be in the barn or near the sheep. If Eve was in one of the three fields that surrounded our backyard, she would come running to the fence as soon as she heard Emma's voice if she was playing on the swing set or playing with her older siblings or with the dog—it did not matter. Eve responded to the sound of Emma's voice.

Emma was always quick to reward Eve's loyalty by petting her, hugging her, feeding her a bit of extra corn, and just standing at her side telling her how much she loved her. And each time I witnessed this, I was both amazed and humbled.

I was amazed that a toddler and a sheep had such an automatic connection, that Emma was so capable in gaining Eve's trust, and that Eve was so willing to trust a child.

My amazement turned to humility when I thought about how similar my relationship with God should be to Emma and Eve's relationship.

I thought about the multiple times I had heard God's voice but didn't go running to him like Eve did to Emma. I thought about the times God wanted to comfort me, reassure me, and lead me, but I didn't come close enough to get the full benefit of his love and wisdom the way Eve was always willing to come beside Emma. The greatest impact Emma and Eve's connection had on my spiritual life, however, came the day I needed *three-year-old* Emma's help to move the sheep.

Now, before you start looking up child labor laws to send me, you need to a) let me explain and b) understand that farming really is a family affair.

Anyway, I needed to move the sheep to a different pasture. So after telling Emma to play on the swing set, I headed to the barn.

The sheep were familiar with the routine and trusted me completely, so this little chore usually didn't take more than a few minutes. But because Emma was visible to Eve, Eve wouldn't come with the rest of the sheep. Even though I knew she would still be able to see Emma in the other field, Eve didn't have the ability to figure this out, so she simply refused to come. Until, that is, I had Emma join me in leading the sheep through the gate.

I'm not going to lie. I was more than a bit frustrated at first. But then it hit me: God was trying to teach me that I needed to be as committed to listening to him and as in tune to his voice as Eve was to the voice of my sweet little Emma. God reminded me that by keeping our eyes and ears glued to him, we will never have to worry about having what we need, being where we need to be, and doing what we were created to do. He really *is* the way, truth, and life.

Emma and Eve shared over ten more years of a loyal and loving friendship before Eve died at a ripe old age. In that time, Eve provided Emma with lambs from which she was able to build her own flock of sheep to care for and profit from.

Mercifully, our relationship with God doesn't ever have to end the way Emma and Eve's did. We can have an eternity to enjoy a loving and faithful relationship with our Savior and Shepherd. All we have to do is look for him, listen for his voice, and follow.

Additional Scriptures of Encouragement

He said to them, "Take to heart all the words I have solemnly declared to you this day, so that you may command your children to obey carefully all the words of this law. They are not just idle words for you – they are your life.
~Deuteronomy 32:46–47a NIV

Whether you turn to the right or to the left, your ears will hear a voice behind you, saying, "This is the way; walk in it." ~Isaiah 30:21 NIV

For the word of God is alive and active. Sharper than any double-edged sword, it penetrates even to dividing soul and spirit, joints and marrow; it judges the thoughts and attitudes of the heart.
~Hebrews 4:12 NIV

About the Author

Darla Noble's love of writing began in the fourth grade after meeting (then) up-and-coming children's author Judy Blume, who autographed her copy of *Are You There, God…It's Me, Margaret.*

For over twenty years, now, Darla has been working as an author, freelance writer, and ghostwriter for over twenty years. She specializes in devotionals, Christian parent/family resources, Bible studies, preschool and elementary curriculum, and historical nonfiction.

In addition to *Through the Eyes of a Shepherd,* you are sure to enjoy Darla's other books which include:

Love, Momma D: a collection of stories based on Darla's 'adventures' as a mom and nanna.

Each story reminds us that raising our children with unconditional love is the greatest and most important gift we can give them.

All My love, George…Letters from a WWII Hero is a collection of letters written by Army medic, George Burks. The letters, as well as the thoughts and memories of George's younger brother, tell the story of an American hero who paid the ultimate price for our freedom. This book is a must-read for every American.

Faith is Like Chocolate, a devotional book, will be released in early 2018. Each and every page will remind you of just how personally interested God is in YOUR life.

Darla Noble has been happily married to her high school sweetheart, John, for thirty-seven years. They are the proud parents of four grown children and Nanna and Grandpa to seven nearly-perfect grandchildren. When she isn't writing, Darla enjoys gardening and camping.